W9-AWJ-534

WRITE HERE

Ideas, activities and bulletin boards
to spark creative writing

by
Joanne Richards
and
Marianne Standley

Incentive Publications, Inc.
Nashville, Tennessee

Cover illustration by Becky Cutler

ISBN 0-86530-013-5

TABLE OF CONTENTS

INTRODUCTION

WRITE HERE is designed for the teacher in need of stimulating creative writing ideas, center materials, bulletin boards and related activities. These ideas lend themselves to self-directed or teacher-directed projects that fit individual classroom needs.

Each activity includes suggestions for motivating students, materials needed, display ideas and adaptations for other subject areas. All illustrations may be reproduced on transparencies with the use of a copying machine.

The ideas in this book offer a springboard for the creative teacher. They have been classroom tested. Since the activities vary in degree of time needed for preparation, they can be easily incorporated into any classroom situation and suited to individual teaching styles.

WRITE A SCOOPER- DOOPER STORY

Write a "scooper-dooper story" and lick the writing blues! Your stories will be the cream of the crop, chock-full of the flavor of creativity.

SUGGESTED MOTIVATIONS
- Discuss the different flavors of ice cream, especially unusual combinations such as pineapple-cranberry, peanut-pumpkin, or prune ripple.
- Bring in lists from local ice-cream parlors and discuss the flavors.
- Make homemade ice cream in class. Enjoy!

STORY STARTERS
- Yesterday, while I was at the ice-cream parlor, there was a terrible explosion and . . .
- Remember the time we made homemade ice cream? When we stopped cranking, we peeked inside the freezer and, oops!
- I'll never forget the time I fell head over heels into the barrel of bubble gum ice cream!
- I ate so much ice cream last night that I had a horrible nightmare. Let me tell you about it.
- Do you know why banana split?
- As I leaned over the railing, my ice cream fell from its cone right onto . . .

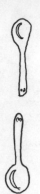

- I licked my crunchy Rocky Road ice cream. Boy, was it good! But no matter how much I licked, it wouldn't disappear. No wonder! They used real rocks!
- The flavor of the month is what?
- The day I climbed ice-cream mountain, . . .

SUGGESTED MATERIALS AND DIRECTIONS

hot pink background

lime green caption

white for hat, collar and cuff

red for bow tie

gray for scooper

tan for cones

green poster for island

slit

assorted pastels for scoops of ice cream

1. Write the story starters on the backs of ice creams.
2. Make slits for cones in the island. See illustration.
3. Insert the cones in the slits.

ADAPTATIONS

- **Social Studies:** Discover when ice cream was first served to the public.

  Locate Coney Island on a New York map. Research the island in relation to its history as an amusement park.

- **Science:** Discover the reason ice cream freezes.

- **Health:** Compute the caloric count in various kinds of ice cream (dietetic vs. regular or sherbet).

  Find the food values contained in ice cream.

THE QUILT PATCH

Get all wrapped up in your writing and piece together a story that will keep your class in stitches.

SUGGESTED MOTIVATIONS

- Play the recording of "Grandma's Feather Bed" by John Denver.
- Display quilts or quilt squares of different patterns.

STORY STARTERS

- When I planted my garden this year, I did something a little different. I decided to plant a quilt patch.
- Aunt Tillie's old quilt kept me in stitches last night with the tale it told me.
- I know this funny bee that doesn't make honey. He makes quilts instead. Naturally, they call him the quilting bee.

- Now I know why they call this quilt pattern "out of this world." Every time I go to sleep . . .

- I never knew what an "undercover agent" was until I peeked under the quilt. You'd never guess what I saw!

SUGGESTED MATERIALS AND DIRECTIONS

black caption

striped background (wrapping paper or wallpaper)

brown tag for bed

manila tag for pillows

white for quilt and red for crossbars and binding

multi-colors for flowers and yellow for flower centers

yellow for girl's hair

manila for girl's face, hands and feet

blue for rug

yellow and orange for cat

1. Write one story starter in the center of each of six flowers.

ADAPTATIONS
- **Social Studies:** Research quilt patterns and the reasons for their names.
- **Math:** Estimate yardage and cost to make quilts for different sized beds.
- **Art:** Make a classroom quilt. Each student makes a square depicting an event unique to him or her.

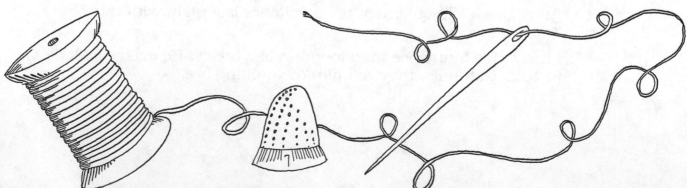

HANG BY A SWINGING TALE

Don't monkey around with writing. Use these story starters to help your students write some swinging tales!

SUGGESTED MOTIVATIONS
- Provide pictures of different kinds of jungle animals, especially monkeys. Discuss the physical characteristics, habitats and diets of each.
- Provide each student with a lined monkey page to be used for the final copy of the story.

STORY STARTERS
- I was watching an old Tarzan movie on TV, when suddenly Cheetah swung out on a vine and grabbed me by the hand. The next thing I knew . . .
- A lion's ferocious roar found me armed only with a camera!
- People love to look at me in my cage! But look at all the fun I have. I'm a people watcher! Why, just the other day . . .
- I've heard of monkey business, but this is ridiculous! This monkey is the owner of . . .

- Due to a severe winter, King Kong has moved South and finds himself in need of a job. These are his qualifications:
  1. vine swinger
  2. office building climber
  3. accurate pitcher (bats .500 with airplanes)

Write a conversation between King Kong and a prospective employer.

SUGGESTED MATERIALS AND DIRECTIONS

brown kraft paper or paper bags for caption

blue background

green for vines

brown kraft paper or paper bags for monkeys

black for boots and camera

white for safari suit and pith helmet

manila tag for speech bubbles

1. Drape vines loosely across the board.
2. Hang monkeys from the vines.
3. Write story starters on speech bubbles.
4. Place speech bubbles near characters.

ADAPTATIONS

- **Science:** Have students research and find out exactly what monkeys can do that humans can do too.
- **Art:** Make a jungle mural.
- **Life Skills:** Using job applications from local stores and fast-food chains, have students complete applications as though King Kong or Curious George were seeking employment.

THIS ADS UP

Advertise your kids' abilities to write snappy sentences with this totally new idea!

SUGGESTED MOTIVATIONS
- Discuss idioms and multiple meanings of words. Explain that some words can be used as different parts of speech.
- Talk about commercial products that have unusual names such as Bold, Treet, Shield and Secret.

SAMPLE SENTENCE STARTER
- *Aunt Clara* felt *instant relief* when, by some *miracle,* she passed the *test* and won everybody's *applause.*
  (See illustration on page 17.)

SUGGESTED MATERIALS AND DIRECTIONS
envelopes, product pictures or labels

1. Make a set of envelopes. Each envelope should contain five or six product pictures or labels.

2. Have students use only one word from each product or label and words of their own to make silly sentences. See the sample sentence starter.

3. Products, pictures and labels interspersed with students' words may be glued to paper for a display.

ADAPTATIONS
- **Language Arts:** Have students create new products of their own. Design labels and write advertisements for these products.

- **Math:** Have students watch TV for a designated hour, both morning and night. Tally and graph the kinds of products advertised.

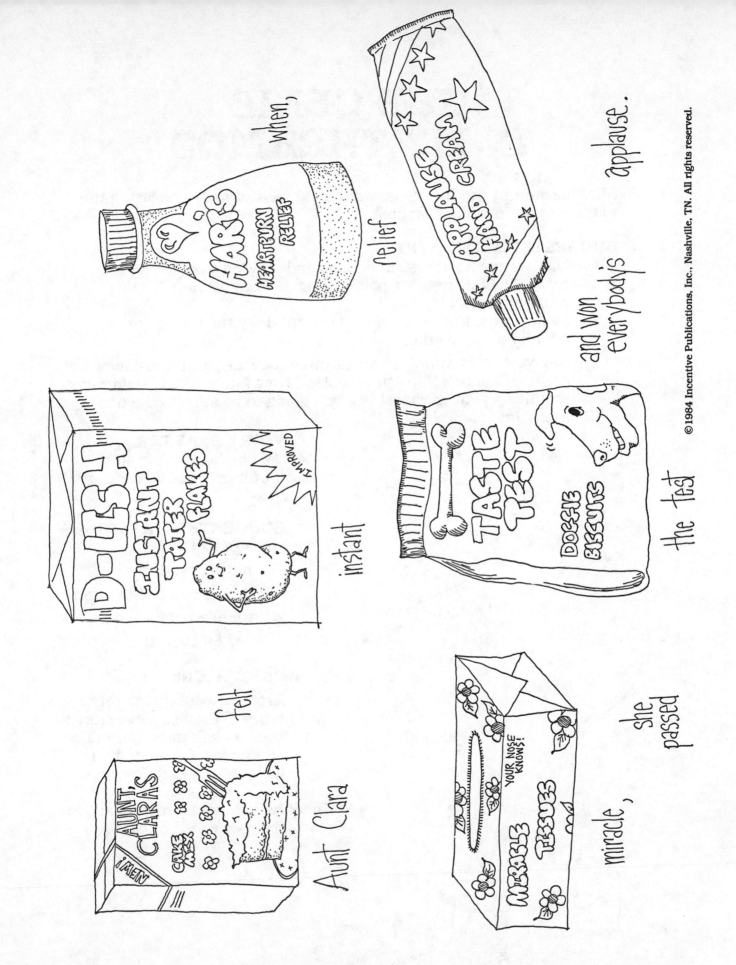

when,

relief

and won everybody's   applause.

instant

the test

felt

Aunt Clara

miracle,   she passed

by   some

17

THE GENIE IN MY THERMOS

Shazaaaaammmm! This genie will quickly assist you in releasing the magic in your students' writing.

SUGGESTED MOTIVATIONS
- Discuss magic, unusual lunches and making wishes.
- Read Shel Silverstein's poem, 'Magic,' from "Where The Sidewalk Ends."
- Make a tape from the following script. Play the tape as an additional motivation.

(Big yawn) Ho-hum! I've spent three thousand years inside of one bottle or another. (splashing noises) Now I find myself swimming around in your thermos! Are you going to be surprised when lunchtime comes!

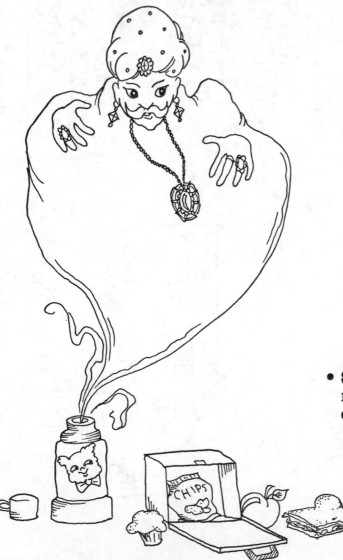

STORY STARTER
Use the tape as the story starter or read the script to the class.

SUGGESTED MATERIALS AND DIRECTIONS
purple caption

lime green background

manila tag for genie

red for thermos

ADAPTATIONS
- **Literature:** Explore other types of make-believe stories such as folk tales, fairy tales and fables. Compare their likenesses and differences.

- **Speech:** Students might want to read their stories to younger classes.

WRITE A T-RRIFIC STORY

Try these story starters for shirt-tales that will suit you to a "T."

SUGGESTED MOTIVATIONS
- Have students bring in old T-shirts and decorate them with fabric markers. Emphasize self-expression and personality in designs.
- Discuss T-shirts as social commentaries.

STORY STARTERS
- Last night I ironed a transfer of _____ on my new T-shirt. But when I put it on, I felt something seeping through to me. Oh no, it . . .

- Batman puts on his T-shirt and ta-daaa! Superman puts on his T-shirt and ta-daaa! I put on my T-shirt and aaagh!

- When you consider all I have to go through, being a T-shirt is not all that easy. First, . . .

- Drip! Drop! Drip! Drop! Boy, that rain is something else. My T-shirt got wet and it's shrinking. Oh no, I am too!

- I'll never forget it as long as I live — the day my T-shirt transfer came to life!

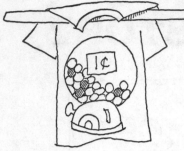

SUGGESTED MATERIALS AND DIRECTIONS

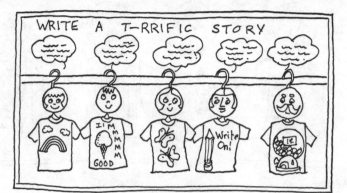

black caption

orange background

brown for clothes pole

black for hanger tops

manila tag for speech bubbles

blue for rainbow shirt

hot pink for ice-cream shirt

yellow for butterfly shirt

tan for pencil shirt

green for bubble gum shirt

assorted colors for details on shirts

1. Write the story starters on the speech bubbles.

ADAPTATIONS

1. **Art:** Design logos. Tie-dye or silk-screen T-shirts.

2. **Social Studies:** Since most T-shirts are 100% cotton, have students research cotton growing and processing.

   Make a map of cotton-producing states using T-shirts to mark the important cities.

3. **Values:** Design your own T-shirt to show how you feel about yourself, your school or _____ .

HOP TO IT AND WRITE!

Let stories mushroom in your classroom! Get set with writing pads and leap into those story starters. It only takes a tad of imagination. I "toad" you so!

SUGGESTED MOTIVATIONS
- Read the fairy tale "The Frog Prince" to the class.
- Discuss the evolution of frogs from the tadpole stage to the frog stage. Emphasize speed and jumping ability.

STORY STARTERS
- Aaay! I am Fonzie Frog! I live in a cool pad. In order to prove how cool I am, the other day I . . .
- My name is Alfred. Yesterday, I found this bottle on my lily pad. When I drank from it, I went through the looking pond and . . .
- Hi! I'm really the prince who kissed the wrong girl. Instead of turning into a regular frog, I turned into an invisible frog. That's not all bad because . . .
- I am A. J. Frog, winner of the Lake 500 and the owner of the fastest lotus leaf west of the Mississippi! In one of my races, I . . .

- You guessed it! I am a yellow frog and all the others are green with envy! I became yellow when . . .

- I am Superfrog! Able to leap tall cattails with a single bound and faster than a speeding tadpole! Nothing has ever been impossible for me, except the time that . . .

- I am Santa Frog and have a case of the measles! This has its advantages since it's Christmas. My red spots are mixed with my green and now I can . . .

SUGGESTED MATERIALS AND DIRECTIONS

black caption

blue pond

green frogs, grass, and lily pads

lime green for frogs' stomachs

brown for cattails and diving board

orange mushroom

1. Write the story starters on the backs of lily pads.
2. Place seven strips of nylon adhesive on the water.
3. Attach a strip of the adhesive material to the top back of each lily pad.

ADAPTATIONS
- Find out the differences between toads and frogs.
- Read "frog" books like "Wind in the Willows," or "Frog and Toad Together."
- For older students, read Mark Twain's "The Celebrated Jumping Frog of Calaveras County." Have a frog jumping contest and award prizes.

LOST & FOUND

Has your class lost touch with writing skills lately? Find new confidence with ideas that can "ad" up!

SUGGESTED MOTIVATIONS

- Read the lost and found ads in the classified section of your local newspaper. Note unusual items that have been lost or found. Note the rewards offered as well.

- Discuss unusual things your students have lost or found and the circumstances accompanying the events.

STORY STARTERS

- Coin Purse — I discovered I'd lost my money just as the bill came in the restaurant. HELP!

- Notebook — After I forgot to do my homework three days in a row, my teacher wrote Mom one last note in my assignment book. On the way home, I dropped it in the downpour and the note washed off. Who's going to believe me now?

- Ring — I was helping Mom scoop ice for the snow cones at the school carnival when I noticed the diamond missing from the ring Grandma had given me. Now what?

- Lunch Box — Ham sandwich, corn chips, lemonade and cupcakes! What a neat lunch! Yuck! What happened? Zucchini sticks, fried egg sandwich, yogurt bars and cranberry juice? Who switched my lunch? What? Yours too? And yours? Ms. _____ (teacher's name) _____!

GIGGLE GIGGLE • TEE HEE • HO HO • HA HA • HEE HEE

- Shoe — I slipped my shoes off at the banquet table. When I started to get up to leave, I discovered someone had kicked them under another table. What do I do?

- Pocketbook — I found this neat box on the way to register here at (school). When it was our turn to talk to the principal, Mom said, "What do you have there? Give it to me." She put it in her purse. Later, she reached into her purse to get my old report card as the principal said, "Do you think you'll like it here? You certainly have a well-behaved little son/daughter." Just then, the box tipped over and all we heard was ho-ho-ho-hee-hee-hee-tee-hee-giggle-giggle. What would you do?

SUGGESTED MATERIALS AND DIRECTIONS

1. Cover a box and its lid with adhesive paper.

2. Label the box "Lost & Found."

3. Collect the following items:
   - coin purse
   - notebook
   - ring
   - lunch box
   - shoe
   - pocketbook

4. Glue copies of story starters to luggage tags.

5. Attach the tags to appropriate items and place in box.

ADAPTATIONS

- **Language Arts:** Have each student choose an article from the school's lost and found box. Have each student write a "Dear Abby" letter from the lost articles ("I'm a red sweater and I'm lost . . .").

  Have students bring in the lost and found ads from local newspapers. Have them write character studies of the persons who might own such items.

- **Study Skills:** Sort and classify items in the school's lost and found box. Have students chart the items most frequently lost.

WRITING — RAIN OR SHINE

Come rain or shine, your students will weather writing when you shower them with these ideas!

SUGGESTED MOTIVATIONS

- Discuss the mythology and biblical references concerning rain and rainbows.

- Play "Raindrops Keep Falling On My Head" by B.J. Thomas.

- Recall childhood songs and games involving rain (Rain, Rain Go Away; It's Raining, It's Pouring, etc.).

STORY STARTERS

- Now I know what the salt people meant by "when it rains it pours." It's raining salt! Just think of the possibilities!

- Have you heard the story of the beach umbrella that got sunburnt? Well, let me tell you.

- My Chinese parasol is magical. It's made of beautifully colored paper and fragile wood. I opened it during a downpour and each raindrop mysteriously became a tiny rainbow. There were millions of rainbows!

- Daddy loaned me his push-button umbrella. I had to use it and guess what happened?

- My owner's cart is being replaced by a truck. I've been the only horse on this street corner for a long time and could tell you lots of stories about the things the vendor and I have seen.

- Most things shrink when they're wet, but this raindrop inflated! It got bigger, and bigger, and bigger until . . .

- Have you ever thought of what would happen if rain were invisible?

SUGGESTED MATERIALS AND DIRECTIONS
umbrella

blue for raindrops

white for cloud

yarn, ribbon or string

1. Make one raindrop for each story starter. Punch a hole in the small end of the raindrop and thread yarn, ribbon or string through the hole. Attach the free end of each string to a rib of the umbrella. See illustration.

2. Write the name of the activity on the cloud.

3. Attach yarn, ribbon or string to the top of the umbrella.

4. Punch holes in the top and bottom of the cloud. See illustration. Thread the umbrella string through the holes in the cloud.

5. Suspend the open umbrella as a mobile so that the raindrops hang down.

ADAPTATIONS
- **Art:** Use a color wheel to help discuss the spectrum of the rainbow.

- **Science:** Collect samples of rainwater and examine the drops under a microscope.

- **Social Studies:** Research the origin and the uses of umbrellas.

  In the study of community helpers, take a class field trip to the local weather station or have a weather forecaster as a guest speaker.

THE UPPER CRUST

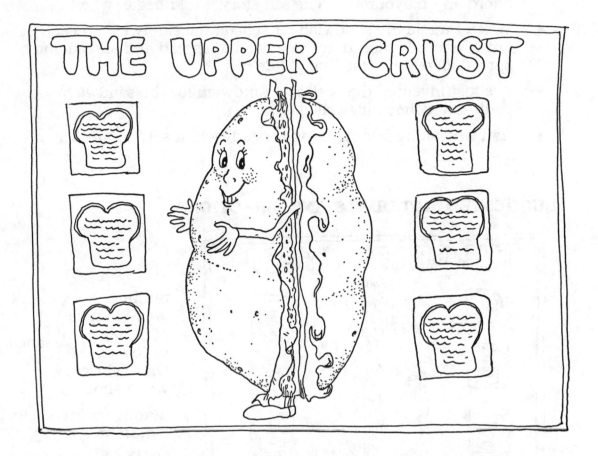

If your students have been loafing when it comes to writing, sandwich these ideas into your creative classes.

SUGGESTED MOTIVATIONS
- Read Shel Silverstein's 'Recipe for a Hippopotamus Sandwich' and/or 'Peanut - Butter Sandwich,' both from "Where the Sidewalk Ends."
- Display menus from fast-food chains, advertisements depicting types of sandwiches or cookbooks with sandwich recipes.

STORY STARTERS
- I started to bite into my submarine sandwich, when I saw a tiny periscope looking me straight in the eye. Who would live in a submarine sandwich? A hero? Somebody full of bologna? Not at all. It was . . .
- I ordered a club sandwich, but I couldn't eat it. Every bite was interrupted by the club meeting going on inside. The members were meeting to . . .

- I felt so sorry for my poor-boy sandwich. It was even too poor to afford any mayonnaise. The sad story it told began when . . .

- When I made my sandwich for school, the sandwich spread got out of hand. It caused my sandwich to spread and spread and spread all over! What should I do?

- I've just invented the best new sandwich for the sandwich contest at school. It's called . . .

- As I was biting into my tongue sandwich, it said to me, " . . .

SUGGESTED MATERIALS AND DIRECTIONS

black caption

tan bun
green lettuce
pink ham } sandwich
yellow cheese
white gloves
white shoes

manila for bread story starters

six sandwich bags

1. Write the story starters on manila bread.
2. Place a story starter in each sandwich bag. Secure the bags to the bulletin board.

ADAPTATIONS
- **Social Studies:** Research the Earl of Sandwich.
- **Math:** Using motivational advertisements, have students calculate the costs of different kinds of sandwiches.

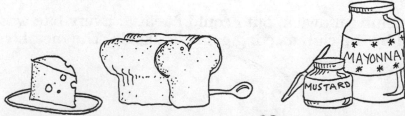

PUT YOURSELF IN OUR SHOES

Step right up to good writing! Get off on the right foot and make tracks with these story starters!

SUGGESTED MOTIVATIONS

- Have each student trace his or her own foot on construction paper. Hang the footprints and have contests to find the longest foot, widest foot, flattest foot or foot with the highest arch.

- List all of the things that feet can do such as sports activities, dancing and locomotion.

STORY STARTERS

- Boy, the other day I shined my shoes so bright, I could see myself in them. But when I looked, I didn't see me at all. Instead, I saw . . .

- Puff! Puff! Puff! I've got these track shoes on and they won't stop making me run. I've got to get them off, but how can I stop to remove them?

- Oh my gosh! I spilled bleach on my feet and they disappeared! That's right, they're invisible! I've got to replace my shoes since the bleach ate them up. How can I do that with invisible feet? How will I ever explain this to the shoe clerk?

29

- I just bought these new stretch socks, but when I put them on, my feet started stretching too!

- I am really down on my luck. I heard that horseshoes bring good luck, but how will I ever talk a horse out of his shoes? I know, . . .

- The strangest thing happened this morning. I woke up and instead of my own feet, I had kangaroo feet! Well, I guess they'll be good for running and soccer, but they're not too handy for climbing stairs! And the teachers say I have to put my shoes on, no matter what! How will I ever explain this to the principal?

- Drip, drip, drip! My feet sure got wet in that rain. Oh no! They shrank!

- I just put these shoes on and I already have a problem. They refuse to take me where I need to go. Instead, . . .

SUGGESTED MATERIALS AND DIRECTIONS

green caption

yellow background

blue denim for jeans

brown for men's boots

red and white checked fabric for skirt

white eyelet for petticoat

red for lady's shoes

two shoe boxes covered in red and white checked adhesive paper

1. Trace eight "foot" shapes on manila tag.
2. Write one story starter on each foot shape.
3. Place the foot shapes in the shoe boxes.

ADAPTATIONS

- **Language Arts:** Brainstorm and discuss idioms concerning feet (get a foothold, land on your feet, put your best foot forward).

- **Study Skills:** Research the use of the foot in measurement.

- **Social Studies:** Discover traditional footwear of other countries.

IN THE SWIM

Fishing for a "reel" good story? Students are sure to take the bait with these story starters!

SUGGESTED MOTIVATIONS

- Read "Swimmy" by Leo Lioni. Note the illustrations as well as the text.
- Share Brian Wildsmith's "Fishes."
- Display a classroom aquarium.

STORY STARTERS

- I'm a goldfish and I'm the wealthiest fish of all.
- Eloise the electric eel moonlights. She turns herself into neon signs. Just the other day, . . .
- I tried to convince the fisherman to throw me back. He fell for my story hook, line and sinker.
- I thought "fish out of water" was only an old saying. Then I met Fiorello, the flying fish. Instead of a high wire act, he . . .
- Sir Sidney Swordfish is at it again! This time he's taking on . . .
- Holy Mackerel really keeps us in line. Even the devilfish leaves him alone. We call him "Holy" because . . .

- You've heard of a "school of fish." Down here we have a riding academy with the sea horse in charge. Heigh-ho!
- I don't mind being a fish, but I hate being in school all day. Maybe I'll play "hooky."

SUGGESTED MATERIALS AND DIRECTIONS

green caption

multicolors for fish

green for seaweed

sandpaper for ocean floor

plastic wrap for bubbles

1. Write one story starter on each fish.
2. Arrange the fish and the seaweed on the board.

ADAPTATIONS

- **Language Arts:** As a follow-up activity, read "Lucy and the Merman."

  Research the folklore and mythology involving the ocean (Neptune, mermaids, mermen, Davy Jones' locker).

- **Health:** Research the uses of algae and kelp as nutritional additives to food.

- **Science:** Discover likenesses and differences between freshwater and saltwater fish.

Letter writing have you in a pickle? This cumbersome task can be sweetened with these story starter letters. Choose your dilly, and relish the results!

IN A PICKLE

SUGGESTED MOTIVATIONS

- Read "Alexander and the Terrible, Horrible, No-Good, Very Bad Day" by Judith Viorst.
- Discuss idioms for being in trouble (in a jam, in a pickle, up a tree, in hot water).
- Provide each student with a lined pickle jar for the final copy of the letter.

STORY STARTERS

- The Day I Brushed My Teeth with Denturstay!

  Dear Dr. _____ ,
  The reason my toothbrush is attached to my teeth is . . .

- The Day I Took the Wrong School Bus

  Dear Mrs. Terwilliger,
  The reason you've never seen me in your school before is . . .

- The Day I Wore My Railroad Train Pajamas to School

  Dear Coach,
  I can't dress out for P.E. today because . . .

Q. Cumber's Patch

- The Day I Got Stuck

  Dear Ms. _____ ,
  It looks as if I'll have to take my desk home with me today
  because . . .

- The Day I Wore My Humpty Dumpty Costume a Day Early

  Dear Ms. _____ ,
  I just want you to know I'm going to have trouble sitting down
  today because . . .

SUGGESTED MATERIALS AND DIRECTIONS

large white gummed label
   for jar

green for pickles

white correction fluid
   for eyes

large jar for pickles

1. Write the story starters on the backs of pickles.

2. Place pickles in the jar.

3. Write the teacher's name on the blank of the label.

ADAPTATIONS

- **Speech:** Use story starters for creative dramatics or impromptu
  speeches.

- **Science:** Plant cucumbers as a classroom project and research
  the making of pickles.

I'M IN HOT WATER AGAIN

Let your writing worries go down the drain. Your students will bubble over with these story starters!

SUGGESTED MOTIVATIONS

- Discuss the differences in language usage when speaking to different people (friends, principal, parents).

- Have three students role play a situation in which different viewpoints are involved (a child who gets into a schoolyard fight: his principal, his parents and his peers).

STORY STARTERS

- You invited a new friend to go to the show. Then your best friend invites you to go to _____ . You have always wanted to go there. What do you say to
  - your best friend?
  - your new friend?
  - your parent(s)?

- You have just broken your brother's skateboard. Tell your side of the story to
  - your best friend
  - your brother
  - your parent(s)

36

- You lost your older brother's tickets to _____ . They cannot be replaced.
  What will you say to
    - the box office salesperson?
    - your older brother?
    - your older brother's date?

- You live in an apartment. You put too much soap in your washer and it overflowed and leaked downstairs. What will you say to
    - the apartment manager?
    - your parent(s)?
    - the people who live below you?

- Your little brother just tore up your science project. It is due tomorrow. It took you two weeks to complete it. What will you say to
    - your teacher?
    - your parent(s)?
    - your little brother?

- You have just spent all your money at the amusement park. Then you remember your mother's birthday is tomorrow. What will you say to
    - your mother?
    - your dad, who gives you your allowance?
    - your best friend?

- Make up a problem of your own. Who will you have to explain it to? Write your three sides of the story.

SUGGESTED MATERIALS AND DIRECTIONS

hot pink caption

aqua background

lavender tub

white suds

yellow duck

empty bubble bath and soap boxes

lavender, hot pink, yellow, orange, lime, blue and white "soaps"

1. Write story starters on soap shapes.

2. Insert soap shapes into small soap boxes.

ADAPTATIONS

- **Social Studies:** View current events from the vantage points of differing nations and political leaders.

- **Science:** Find the differences between soap and detergent.

  Have students bring in stained articles of clothing. Experiment to determine proper stain removal.

- **Language Arts:** Make up commercials about soap from the points of view of the manufacturer, consumer and the salesperson. Emphasize the use of propaganda in advertising (snob appeal, plain folks, testimonial).

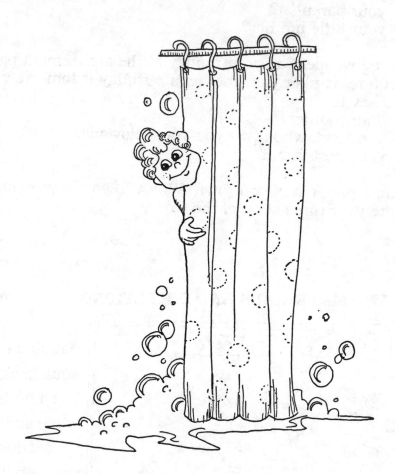

WHAT'S IN A NAME?

Writing is the name of this game! Students will strike a happy medium between plot and setting with these characters.

SUGGESTED MOTIVATIONS

*   Have students find the meaning(s) of their first names.

*   Discuss the meanings and derivations of some of the more common surnames (i.e., Johnson: son of John; Smith: blacksmith).

STORY STARTERS: Have each student choose a name group, assign an occupation appropriate to each name and write a story incorporating all the characters and occupations.

example: Jewel Box: jewelry store owner
Robin Banks: thief
Nick O'Time: policeman
N. A. Cell: prisoner

Roland Rock	Miles Togo
Tom Tom	Don Sneakers
Zane E. Nut	Stan Still
Claire N. Net	Terry Cloth

Doug Deep	Miss Nomer
Dan D. Lion	Miss Pelled
Q. Cumber	Miss N. Formed
Up C. Daisy	Miss L. Toe
E. Z. Rider	Ida Know
Seymour Road	Ima Goldbrick
Phil R. Up	Wanda Cupacoffee
Wade N. Water	Crystal Ball
M. U. Nition	U. R. Ill
Clay Pigeon	I. C. Ewe
Ray Gunn	N. D. Gestion
Al E. Kat	N. Surgery

SUGGESTED MATERIALS AND DIRECTIONS

aqua caption and question marks

yellow background

red and white scarf

green vest and table

multicolored blouse

white tag or poster for crystal ball/black base

1. Write a set of names on the back of each question mark.

2. Place eight strips of nylon adhesive to the board around the fortune teller. See illustration.

3. Attach a strip of the adhesive material on the top back of each question mark.

4. Place the question marks on the board at adhesive.

ADAPTATION

• **Social Studies:** Make family trees.

DIAL-A-STORY

Students can become big time operators in their use of quotation marks if you don't let creative writing be a hang-up. This center is sure to ring a bell with its catchy story lines!

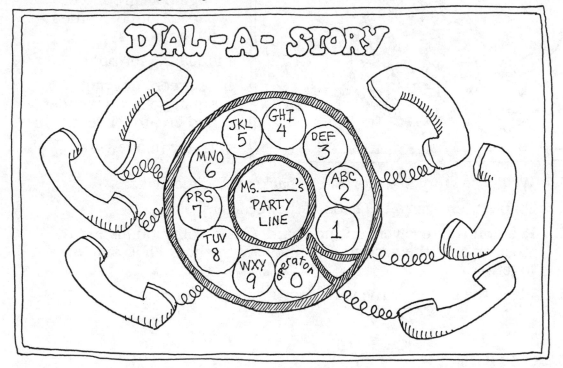

SUGGESTED MOTIVATIONS

- Role play conversations using toy telephones.
- Read a play or an excerpt from a play, noting the dialogue as it becomes conversation.

STORY STARTERS

What did they say to each other?

. . . two cars racing to the same parking space

. . . a blustery wind and a kite snagged on a telephone wire

. . . a sharp razor and a scratchy beard

. . . a feather duster and a shelf full of fragile "whatnots"

. . . a picture post card and an icy mailbox

. . . a hot-air balloon and a Chinese butterfly kite

. . . a grassy lawn and feet that keep stepping on it

. . . an umbrella and a family of raindrops

SUGGESTED MATERIALS AND DIRECTIONS

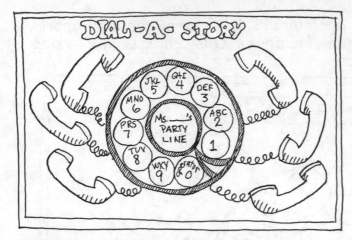

black caption

orange background or pages from discarded phone books

manila tag for phone dial

lime green, hot pink, aqua, yellow, lavender and cream for receivers

yarn for phone wires

1. Write the story starters on the backs of the receivers.
2. Staple the yarn to the ends of the receivers.
3. Position the receivers on the board. (See illustration.) Bring the loose ends of the yarn to the middle of the board and staple together.
4. Place the dial over the yarn ends and staple in place.

ADAPTATIONS

- **Social Studies:** Use these ideas with a unit on community helpers and discuss telephone courtesy.
- **Drama:** Adapt the dialogues for creative drama or mime.
- **Art:** Convert the completed conversations into comic strips.

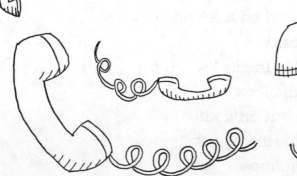

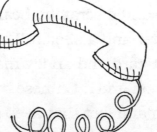

DON'T BE A DING-A-LING. WRITE!

If you liked DIAL-A-STORY, give these ideas a ring!

SUGGESTED MOTIVATION

• This center is intended as a follow up to DIAL-A-STORY.

STORY STARTERS

What did they say to each other?

. . . a pay phone that wants a raise and a caller who is running out of change

. . . a fish and a worm dangling at the end of a hook

. . . a ghost and a house that doesn't want to be haunted

. . . a horse that wants to wear cowboy boots instead of horseshoes and a shoe salesman

. . . thunder and lightning bolts

. . . a bar of soap and dirty hands

. . . a pilot and an airplane that is afraid to fly

. . . a Martian convincing the president to return his UFO

SUGGESTED MATERIALS AND DIRECTIONS

red caption

hot pink background

white poster for phones
black outlining and
features

red poster for lips

white paper insets on
red lips

1. Write the story starters on the white paper insets.

ADAPTATIONS

- **Social Studies:**   Discover different means of communication through the ages (hieroglyphics, smoke signals, sign language).

    Look up methods of communicating emergency situations (Morse code SOS, Mayday, flag upside down, emergency flares, etc.).

- **Creative Drama:**   Play charades to communicate the story starters.

- **Language Arts:**   Become better acquainted with idioms related to communication (give lip service to, talk big, talk down, double talk, sweet talk, tell tales out of school, talk through your hat, tell it like it is, talk is cheap).

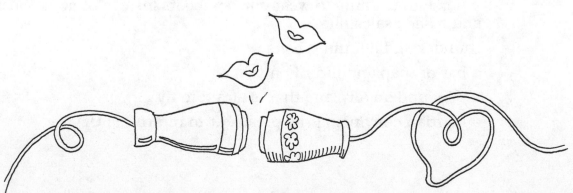

STORIES UP OUR SLEEVES

Would you give your right arm for a good story? Then roll up your sleeves and get started on these story starters.

SUGGESTED MOTIVATIONS

- Discuss the different meanings of coats (overcoats, coat of paint, coat of arms, coati-mundi).
- Discuss coats as distinguishing features of special people (Superman's cape, a magician's tails, the detective's cape).

STORY STARTERS

- While up in the attic, I discovered Grandma's old fur neckpiece. When I tried it on, I think it tried to bite me! Good grief! Is this thing still alive?
- While making a phone call from the booth on the corner, I found a cape tucked down behind the phone book. I threw it over my shoulders and became . . .
- I went to the magic show and when the magician stepped into the spotlight, he said the wrong magic words. The tails on his coat began to grow! What a tale he could tell!
- While waiting for the doctor, I tried on his extra white coat. WOW! Everybody in the waiting room looks like a skeleton!
- I put on my windbreaker and lo and behold! It broke up the wind into little pieces! How do I put it back together?
- When I put on my raincoat, I get even wetter than when I don't wear it! This raincoat rains! I make a big splash wherever I go.

while up in the attic, I . . .

Stories Up Our Sleeves

SUGGESTED MATERIALS AND DIRECTIONS

manila tag for hands and arms, solid fabric for cuffs, printed fabric for sleeves, buttons, one-pound coffee can

1. Use a one-pound coffee can for the container. Cover the bottom four inches of the can with printed fabric. Cover the remainder of the can to the top with solid fabric as a cuff. Glue one button on the cuff.

2. Use the pattern to make six hands and arms.

3. Cover the arm area of the tag with printed fabric as a sleeve. Cover the cuff area with solid fabric. Glue a button in place.

4. Write story starters on the palms of the hands.

5. Place story starters in the can.

ADAPTATIONS

- **Social Studies:** Research the reasons coats have buttons.

- **Art:** Create an occupation and design a coat for it. The teacher may have students trace each other's bodies on kraft or butcher paper and draw the designed coats on these figures.

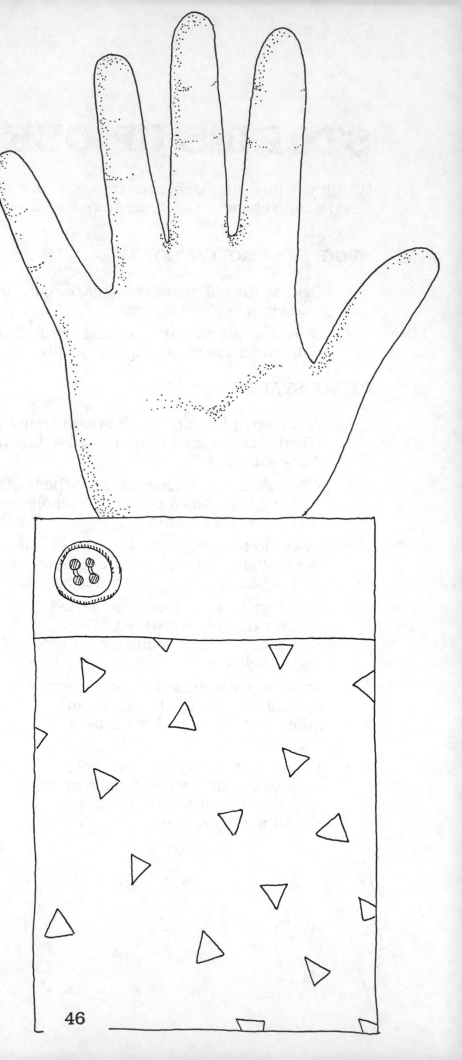

46

TAKE COVER AND WRITE

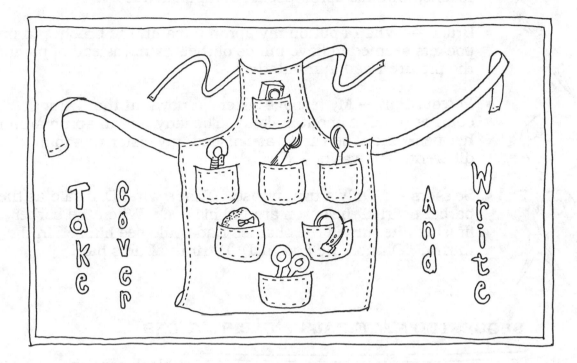

It's time to take an overall approach to writing. Cut the apron strings and turn your students loose with these ideas!

SUGGESTED MOTIVATION

* Discuss occupations which require special wearing apparel and tools.

STORY STARTERS

* Spoon — Look what's cookin'! All the food the chef spilled on his apron ran together and created this fantastic new dish! Let me share this recipe with you!

* Wrench — All the tools in the workman's apron secretly decided to trade jobs. The screwdriver thinks he's a pair of pliers and the hammer wants to be a wrench. And that's only the beginning!

* Camera — Look what's developed! When the photographer donned his apron and began to develop the film, all the pictures enlarged. The darkroom is bulging at the seams and the photographer is trapped!

- Horseshoe — When the racehorse came to the blacksmith for new shoes, he requested some with more speed. The blacksmith reached into his apron pocket and pulled out . . .

- Brush — When I put on my apron to paint, the brushes in my pockets seemed to have minds of their own. Instead of painting the picture I had in mind, they . . .

- Powder Puff — My teenage sister sat down at the cosmetic counter to learn about makeup. The lady put an apron around her neck; and when she was finished, my sister was totally different. She was now . . .

- Scissors — "Only a trim please." That's what Dad said as the barber swirled the apron around his neck. When the barber finished, he turned the chair so Dad could see himself in the mirror. "Oh no!" He had ADDED trim to Dad's hair!

SUGGESTED MATERIALS AND DIRECTIONS

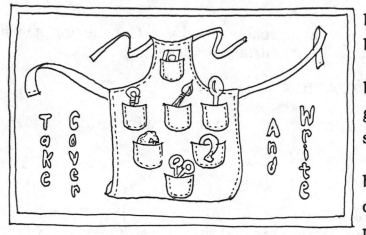

black caption

blue denim for apron and pockets

brown for spoon

gold for horseshoe

silver for wrench and scissors

black for camera

orange for brush

pink for powder puff

1. Write the story starters on the backs of objects.
2. Place the objects in the pockets of the work apron.

ADAPTATION

- **Social Studies:** Use with a unit on community helpers.

UNREAL ESTATE

Tired of building castles in the air? Get a new lease on writing skills with this jiffy idea!

SUGGESTED MOTIVATIONS

- Discuss how shells, trinkets and other unusual items were once used as money.

- Display different kinds of shells.

- Provide each student with a lined sand castle for the final copy of the story.

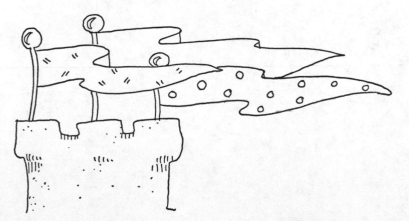

STORY STARTER

I built a sand castle at the beach last weekend. I rented it to
_____ . They paid their rent with _____ and
moved in. Then, . . .

SUGGESTED MATERIALS AND DIRECTIONS

brown caption

blue background

dark blue for water

white for whitecaps

brown for castle

tan for sand

gray for shovel

red for pail

yellow for starfish and
   rent sign

assorted colors for flags

1. Write the story starter on the back of the "For Rent" sign.

ADAPTATIONS

* **Science:** Discover the corrosive properties of salt water.
  Discover the preservative properties as well.

* **Art:** Make sand castles.

CAN OF WORMS

Wiggle your way into a good story with these story starters!

SUGGESTED MOTIVATIONS

- Discuss the value of earthworms to gardeners. Bring up the problems the earthworms solve for those who grow things.

- Discuss problems that seem to have no solutions. Include the definition of a problem.

- Provide each student with a set of numbered worms and a lid pattern for the final copy. Also provide students with tall potato chip cans for storing and displaying final copies.

SUGGESTED MATERIALS AND DIRECTIONS

green tag or construction paper for worms, tall potato chip cans for worms, adhesive paper to cover cans

1. Cover all potato chip cans with adhesive paper. Use the pattern to make green paper lids for cans. Pop the paper lids under the plastic lids of the cans.

2. Place story starters in the teacher's can. Each student chooses a story starter from this can.

3. The final copy of the story is written on a set of numbered worms and placed in the student's can.

ADAPTATIONS

- **Science:** Place several worms in an aquarium filled with soil. Have students observe the tunneling process.

- **Language Arts:** Discuss idioms containing worms (early bird catches the worm, worm your way out of this, can of worms, feel like a worm).

  Use as a follow-up to reading, "How To Eat Fried Worms and Other Plays" by Thomas Rockwell.

Winifred Worm is taking lessons from Carlotta Cobra in order to join the snake charmer's act.

While on a field trip to the museum, I pushed this button marked DO NOT TOUCH.

Someone signed my name to the note addressed to . . .

I was afraid to try it!

The UFO circled the school.

When the principal asked me to answer the office phone, I never knew this could happen!

I'll never go fishing again! You should have heard those worms arguing with me about becoming bait!

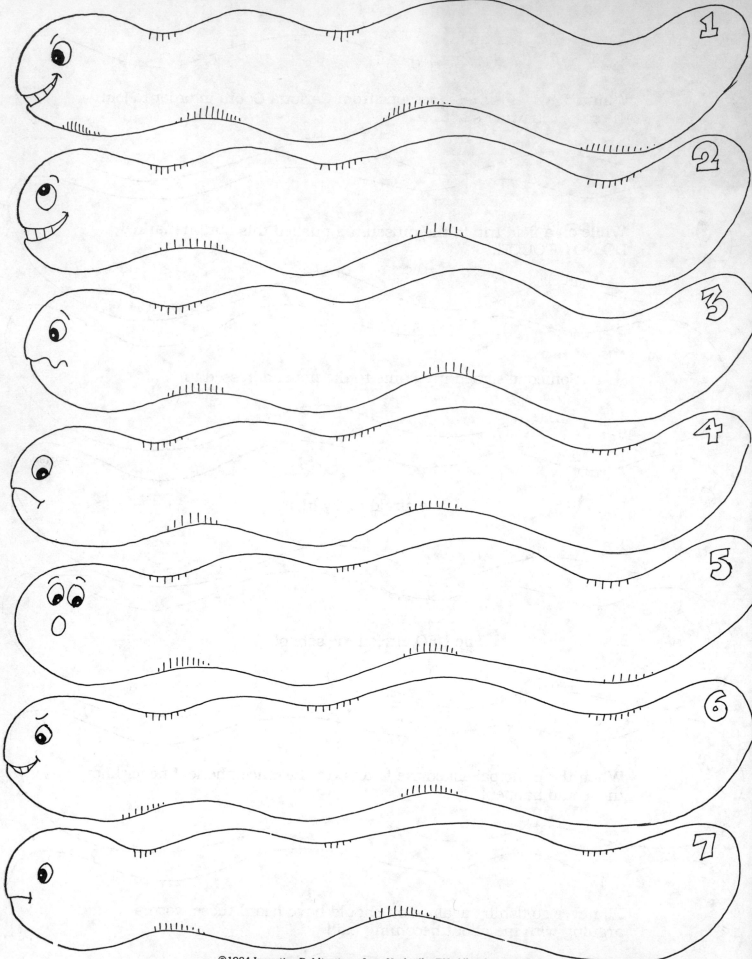

BEAR TALES

Writing hasn't gone to the dogs — it's gone to the bears! These story starters will bear watching in your classroom.

SUGGESTED MOTIVATIONS

- Read students one or more books from "The Little Bear" series by Else Minarik.
- Display Winnie the Pooh cartoon strips from the newspaper.

STORY STARTERS

- Remember "Goldilocks and the Three Bears?" Write a bear tale about Goldibear and the Three People.

- I was so lonely in the forest, I decided to put myself up for adoption. When I went to the A.S.P.C.A. to find a home, . . .

- This bear lost his tracks in a snowstorm and decided to advertise in the newspaper to find them. Write his lost and found ad.

SUGGESTED MATERIALS AND DIRECTIONS

red caption

blue background

black and white for bears

brown for tree stump

green for leaves and grass

white for clouds

yellow for pencils and ribbon

notebook paper

1. Write story starters on notebook paper.

ADAPTATIONS

*   **Social Studies:**   Research the bears of North America. Make a map of the continent, using bear symbols as part of the map's key.

*   **Science:**   Make dioramas displaying bears in their natural habitats.

*   **Language Arts:**   Discuss the idioms containing the word "bear" (bear with me, bear down, bear a cross, bear watching, grin and bear it, bear in mind, grouchy as a bear).

*   **Study Skills:**   Research the origin of the teddy bear.

STORIES TO FIT YOU LIKE A GLOVE

Need a helping hand when it comes to writing? These story starters go hand in glove with creativity!

SUGGESTED MOTIVATIONS

- Have students bring to class various kinds of hand coverings for discussion.
- Discover how hand coverings such as gauntlets, mittens and handcuffs came into use.

STORY STARTERS

- Baseball Mitt — I'm on strike! I refuse to catch any more of those fastballs. Boy! Do they hurt! And I might end up having more stitches! From now on, my owner can just be "out in left field."
- Mittens — Ouch! This football game is really hard on us. My owner keeps clapping us together and it's getting worse and worse. We can't lift a finger to help because we're all thumbs.
- Gauntlet — Oh, for the days of dragons, moats and ladies fair. This corner of the museum is dark, dusty and lonesome. I'm even getting rusty. Wait! What's that I hear?

- Gardening Glove — My owner is so proud of his green thumb, but I do all the work. Wait until he takes me off! His green thumb is permanent!

- Rubber Gloves — Boing! Boing! Boing! Mother was so tired of cleaning, she threw her rubber gloves in the sink and they haven't stopped bouncing yet. Watch out!

SUGGESTED DIRECTIONS AND MATERIALS

red caption

blue background

manila and brown for hands

assorted bright colors for sleeves

1. Write the story starters on the backs of the hands. See illustration.

ADAPTATIONS

- **Math:** Discover the use of the hand as a unit of measurement.

- **Language Arts:** Brainstorm "hand" words (handy, handsome, handicap, handkerchief).

- **Art:** Make thumb print people and animals with ink pads of various colors.

- **Social Studies:** Investigate sign language.

WE'RE ON THE WRITE NOTE

Go on record and write a story! Take note of these story starters and get in the groove! Your students are sure to jump on the bandwagon with noteworthy creations!

SUGGESTED MOTIVATIONS

- Use rhythm band instruments.
- Play records of various instruments. Have students guess the names of instruments they hear.
- Talk about the evolution of sound equipment.

STORY STARTERS

- Have you heard how the drummer played "to beat the band?" Well, it all began when . . .
- Let me tell you about the record that wouldn't stop playing.
- Danny the drummer has a problem. Every time he hits his bass drum, the drumsticks act like boomerangs!
- Here's the story of the first gold record.
- Oliver was a one-man band, until one day all of the instruments, decided to . . .
- Harry blew on his huge tuba, but instead of an oompa, guess what came out?

59

- Henrietta goofed! While playing her harmonica, she inhaled when she should have exhaled! Now, whenever she tries to talk, . . .

- Benny the banjo player tried to string along with his C & W group. But every time he picked his banjo, the banjo picked back and . . .

SUGGESTED MATERIALS AND DIRECTIONS

aqua caption

hot pink background

brown for phonograph base

black for phonograph horn, notes and music lines

white correction fluid or tempera for faces on notes

manila tag for speech bubbles

1. Write the story starters on manila tag.

Sharp teachers might want to use this alternative for display.

- Cover a box with adhesive paper.
- Use black adhesive paper to make the notes and staff.
- Cover a paper towel tube with black adhesive paper. Insert the tube in the box top to hold records.
- Use push pins or medicine bottle caps for controls.
- Trace a 45 r.p.m. record on black tag. Make colored labels on which to write story starters.

ADAPTATIONS

- **Math:**   Poll both students and faculty as to kinds of music preferred. Make a double-bar graph to show the results.
- **Language Arts:**   Write a new verse to a familiar song.
- **Social Studies:**   Research music from foreign countries and make instruments from those lands.

FOOD FOR THOUGHT

Feast your eyes on these tasty ideas. They're sure to whet your students' writing appetites. Create menus for unusual characters in literature, television and the comics.

SUGGESTED MOTIVATIONS

- Provide menus from various restaurants (Chinese, Mexican, fast-food). Classify foods according to taste, smell, color, size, shape, price and texture.

- Discuss words such as brunch, sup, dine, appetizer, beverage, entree, à la carte, continental breakfast, al fresco and progressive dinner.

- Provide each student with a lined menu page to be used for the final copy of menus.

STORY STARTERS

Create a menu for one of more of these characters. Be sure to include as many of the following courses as possible: appetizer, soup, main course, vegetable, bread, salad, beverage and dessert.

Mary Mary Quite Contrary might dine on

deviled eggs
sour pickles
sweet and sour pork
sugar-free lemonade
devil's-food cake

- Dagwood
- Mighty Mouse (cheese lover)
- Jack Sprat (dieter's delight?)
- Casper (clear foods?)
- an exterminator
- George Washington
- Cupid (angelic foods?)
- Spiderman (stringy foods?)

Kermit the Frog might sup on

split green pea soup
frogs' legs
spinach soufflé
lime freeze
grasshopper pie

- a fireman
- Santa Claus
- Snow White
- Humpty Dumpty
- Cinderella
- Johnny Appleseed
- Jack and the Beanstalk
- cartoon characters

SUGGESTED MATERIALS AND DIRECTIONS

black caption

red background or red and white checked tablecloth

white poster for chef's clothes

yellow for food tray

decorative paper plates for story starters

shoe box (covered with adhesive backed paper) for menus

tan for shoes and spoon

1. Write the story starters on the fronts of the paper plates. See illustration.

ADAPTATIONS

- **Math:**   Budget a meal using sample menus.

- **Study Skills:**   Discover origins of food words (sandwich, sirloin steak, peanut).

- **Social Studies:**   Discuss ethnic foods and eating utensils.

- **Health:**   Use the sample menus to devise balanced meals.

- **Language Arts:**   Have students create original stories describing how some foods were named (hero sandwich, grasshopper pie, deviled eggs, crêpes suzette, eggs Benedict and cherries jubilee).

  Using the students' menus from the creative writing activity, devise recipes for listed dishes. Compile these recipes into a class cookbook. Students may research and find recipes or make up their own.

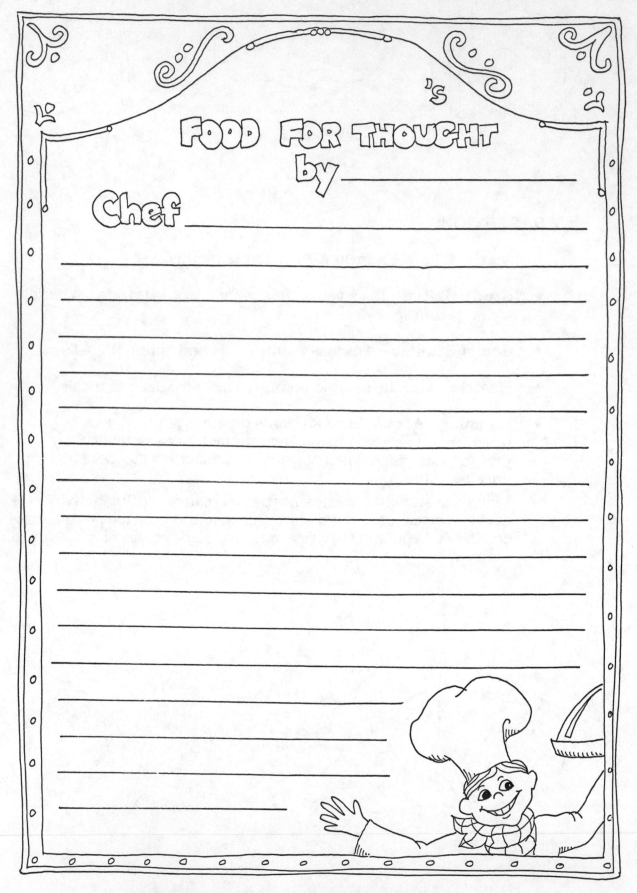

's

FOOD FOR THOUGHT
by _____

Chef _____

_____

_____

_____

_____

_____

_____

_____

_____

_____

_____

_____

_____

_____

WRITE TIME

Make time count with these timely story starters. Your students will spring into action and have the times of their lives!

SUGGESTED MOTIVATIONS

- Read the passage about the White Rabbit and his pocket watch from "Alice in Wonderland" by Lewis Carroll.

- Make a tape of the sounds of various timepieces. Play them for the students and have them match sounds with pictures or examples of the timepieces.

STORY STARTERS

- Wristwatch — I felt a tug on my collar when I held my wrist to my ear. Looking down, I saw the hands on my watch reaching for . . .

- Stopwatch — When the coach punched the button on his stopwatch, everything stopped, even . . .

- Cuckoo — It was time for the cuckoo to come out and announce the hour. Whoops! Something is wrong. The cuckoo seems to have flown the coop, and look who moved in!

- Grandfather Clock — The grandfather clock in the corner is one hundred years old and has seen a lot. I get to see a lot, too. Occasionally, when it strikes the hour, everything in our house goes back a hundred years.

- Sundial — I'm really in the shade when it comes to telling time. I'm up here in the far North where the sun hardly shines. This is a real problem for me. Whenever I must tell the time, I have to . . .

- Alarm Clock — I'm the world's best alarm clock! I take my job seriously. Whenever I go off, all the alarms in town go off too — burglar alarms, fire alarms, you name it!

- Pocket Watch — I'm so cramped in this tiny watch pocket. I'm bursting with tales to tell, if only someone would let me out. I recall the time . . .

- Time Clock — The time clock at work always gives me credit for every bit of work I do. And I do mean credit! When I punch out from work, the clock gives me a different credit card each day.

- Hourglass — Time is running out! The hourglass has sprung a leak and hours, minutes and seconds are escaping. How do you capture time?

SUGGESTED MATERIALS AND DIRECTIONS

black caption

royal blue background

brown for cuckoo and grandfather clocks

grey for time clock, stopwatch and hair

black for watch strap and shoes

gold for pocket watch, wristwatch, hourglass and alarm bells

white for clock faces, sundial and sand in hourglass

green for pants

yellow for cuckoo

red for alarm clock

red and white check for shirt

1. Write story starters on 3x5 inch cards and place under the timepieces. See illustration.

PIPE DREAMS

Students will become effervescent with creativity when they dream up the ending for this story starter.

SUGGESTED MOTIVATIONS

* Allow students to participate in a bubble blowing contest. Decide winners for these categories: the largest bubble, the smallest bubble, the bubble that lasts the longest and the bubble that travels the farthest.

* Provide each student with a lined bubble for the final copy of the story.

STORY STARTER

Once I blew a bubble so big that it surrounded me! It floated up and up with me inside!

SUGGESTED MATERIALS AND DIRECTIONS

black caption	blue background
purple for pipe	white for bubbles
yellow for dress	orange for hair
black for shoes	green for trees
assorted colors for houses	

1. Provide the story starter orally.

67

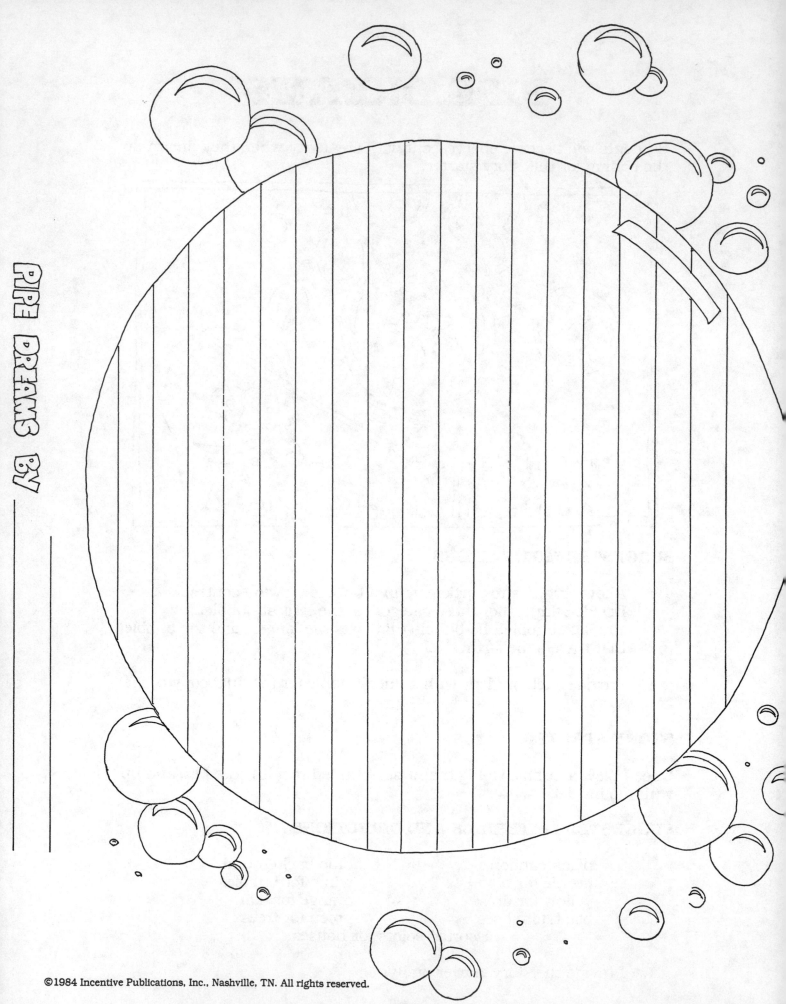

PIPE DREAMS BY

ALL FIRED UP!

Build a fire under your students' writing with these matchless story starters!

SUGGESTED MOTIVATIONS

- Have students collect and bring in matchbooks from various places for display purposes.

- Discover and discuss how matches are made.

STORY STARTERS

- Howdy, pardner. I'm a Shootin' Match!

- I'm the boxing match. My next bout will be with . . .

- My name is Miss Fire, but you can call me Torchy.

- I'd never met my match until I struck up a conversation with . . .

- I've struck it rich! I'm moving into the Matchbox Penthouse. Now I can . . .

SUGGESTED MATERIALS AND DIRECTIONS

red caption

yellow background

lime green for matchbook
   black lettering on
   matchbook

manila tag for match
   bodies

red for match heads

brown for hat, belt and
   holster of Shootin'
   Match

purple shorts for the
   boxing match

hot pink dress and white boa for Miss Fire

yellow dress for the conversationalist

white beads for the rich match

1. Remove matches from five large matchbooks.
2. Write the story starters on the inside of the matchbook covers.
3. Place the covers in a matchbox for kitchen matches.
4. Use a long brad to make a handle for the drawer of the matchbox.

ADAPTATIONS

- **Social Studies:** Research the use of fire and its significance in different cultures.

- **Language Arts:** Write letters to the National Fire Protection Association for literature on fire safety. Address:
      National Fire Protection Association
      Batterymarch Park
      Quincy, MA   02269

- **Science:** Experiment with different methods of extinguishing fire. Place emphasis on different extinguishing methods for various fire causes.

70

HATS OFF
TO GOOD WRITING

Don't keep these ideas under your hat! Get a head start on creativity with these writing goodies!

SUGGESTED MOTIVATION

• Have students make various kinds of hats, using the directions from "Hats Off to Hats!" in the October, 1980 issue of <u>Learning</u> magazine (pgs. 104-105).

STORY STARTERS

• Ski Mask — B-rrrrr. I wore my ski mask to school on a cold day; but when I peeled it off, my face stayed frozen to the mask. How can I get through the day with no face? And how can I get my face back on me?

• Cowboy Hat — This was a ten-gallon hat until someone said, "Hey, Half Pint!" Now I've got a shrinking hat and I don't know what to do.

• Deep Sea Diver Helmet — Glub . . . glub . . . glub . . . I'm diving for treasure deep in the ocean. Suddenly, I realize that a fish is inside my helmet. How do I get him out? I can't resurface yet.

• Ice Pack — This is a switch! My owner had a headache and used me to help him ease the pain. I did such a good job, that now I'm the one with the headache!

- Crown — At my coronation, when the crown was placed on my head, I heard, "Now you are the ruler!" Suddenly, I began to shrink until I was twelve inches high. This is going to be a problem!

- Chinese Worker's Hat — When I put on my Chinese worker's hat for the school play, I found I could only speak Chinese! How will the audience ever understand me?

- Sherlock Holmes Hat — When I put on my Sherlock Holmes detective hat, I realized that I could see out of the back of my head as well as the front. This is great for catching criminals because . . .

- Top Hat — I found a top hat in the attic and decided to wear it in the talent show at school. When it was my turn, I put it on and hundreds of white rabbits came popping out and scampered everywhere! I'm in trouble!

- Dunce Cap — After I sat in the corner for half an hour with the dunce cap on, the teacher told me to take it off and return to my seat. Lo and behold, my head is now pointed too!

SUGGESTED MATERIALS AND DIRECTIONS

black caption
lime green shop caption
hot pink background
lavender hat stands
manila price tags
blue table cover
black top hat
gold crown
yellow Chinese worker's hat
white dunce hat
brown cowboy hat

green helmet
multi-colored ski mask
brown and plaid detective hat

1. Write story starters on price tags and attach to hats with string. See illustration.

PROGRAMMED WRITING

If your students are in outer space when it comes to writing, program them for success with the help of this robot.

Bulletin board text:

YESTERDAY, OUR TEACHER DID NOT FEEL WELL. NOTHING SEEMED TO COMPUTE. IMAGINE OUR SURPRISE THIS MORNING WHEN HER SUBSTITUTE ARRIVED.

A ROBOT!

SUGGESTED MOTIVATIONS

- Discuss the kinds of things you would like robots to do for you.

- Read "Miss Nelson Is Missing" by Harry Allard and James Marshall.

- Provide each student with a copy of the lined robot for the final copy of the story.

STORY STARTER

See bulletin board.

SUGGESTED MATERIALS AND DIRECTIONS

black for chalkboard

red for chalkboard frame and letters for story starter

silver, gold and black for robot

A RAINBOW OF POETRY

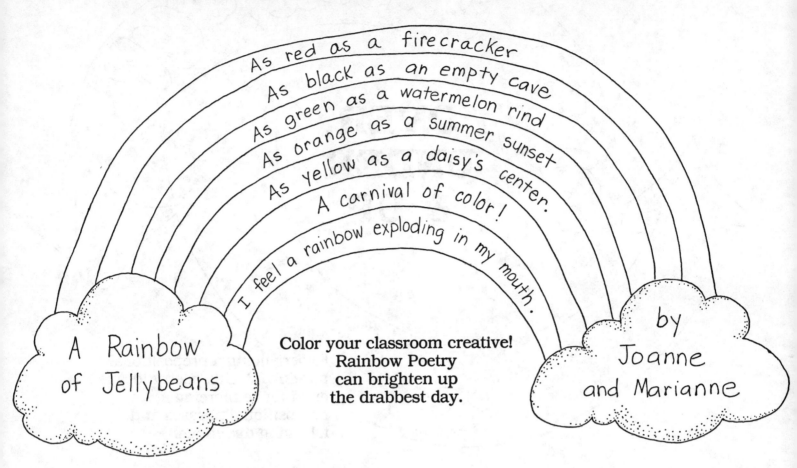

As red as a firecracker
As black as an empty cave
As green as a watermelon rind
As orange as a summer sunset
As yellow as a daisy's center.
A carnival of color!
I feel a rainbow exploding in my mouth.

A Rainbow of Jellybeans

Color your classroom creative!
Rainbow Poetry
can brighten up
the drabbest day.

by Joanne and Marianne

SUGGESTED MOTIVATION
- Read "Hailstones and Halibut Bones" by Mary O'Neill.

SUGGESTED TOPICS
- jellybeans
- flower gardens
- seashells
- thunderstorms
- jigsaw puzzle pieces
- a landscape
- balloons
- butterfly wings
- sunsets
- a basket of fruit

SUGGESTED DIRECTIONS
1. Have students select a topic from the list and five colors that pertain to that topic.
2. Lines 1-5 — Write similes using one of the colors for each line.
3. Line 6 — Write a phrase describing the topic.
4. Line 7 — I feel _____ . (How or what the topic makes me feel).
5. Write the title on the cloud entitled, "A Rainbow of _____ ." The student's name may be written on the other cloud.
6. Suspend rainbows as mobiles.

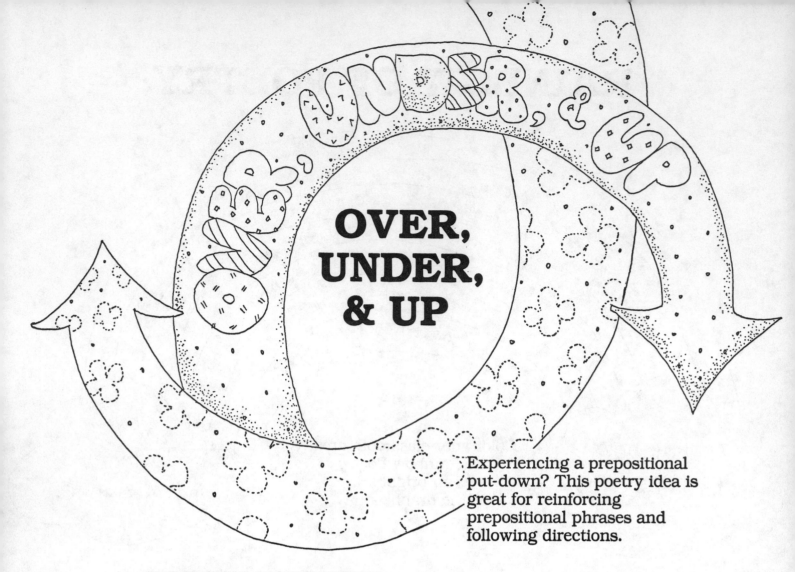

OVER,
UNDER,
& UP

Experiencing a prepositional put-down? This poetry idea is great for reinforcing prepositional phrases and following directions.

SUGGESTED MOTIVATIONS

- Have students contribute to a word bank which includes as many prepositions as possible.

- Display the following example:

                    LINING UP
            Out of my chair
            On the floor
            Across the room
            To the cabinet
            For the balls
            At the door
            In line
            For P.E.
            With my teacher.

SUGGESTED DIRECTIONS

1. Have students choose an activity.
2. Each line of the poem must be a prepositional phrase. Prepositions may be used only once.
3. The completed poem describes an activity from its beginning to its end.

76

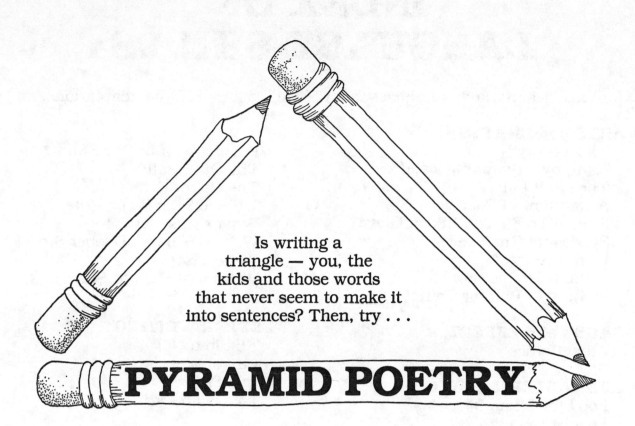

Is writing a triangle — you, the kids and those words that never seem to make it into sentences? Then, try . . .

PYRAMID POETRY

SUGGESTED MOTIVATIONS

- Discuss parts of speech and their usage.
- Discuss the types of questions (who, what, where, when, why and how).
- Display the following example:

Balloons
Patterned and plain
Sail through the skies.
May I join your confettied rainbow?

SUGGESTED DIRECTIONS

1. Have students select a topic.
2. Line 1 — A noun (the topic).
3. Line 2 — Two adjectives describing the noun.
4. Line 3 — A verb plus a prepositional phrase.
5. Line 4 — A question about the noun.
6. Have students write the completed poems on pyramid shapes to display in the classroom.

INDEX OF LANGUAGE SKILLS

Activities marked(*) indicate that the skill is found in the adaptations.

ARTS and CRAFTS
Dial-a-Story*
Hang by a Swinging Tale*
The Quilt Patch*
A Rainbow of Poetry
Stories To Fit You Like a Glove*
Stories up Our Sleeves*
Unreal Estate*
Write a T-rrific Story*
Writing — Rain or Shine*

CAUSE and EFFECT
All activities

CHARACTERIZATION
Food for Thought
Lost & Found*
What's in a Name?

CHARTS and GRAPHS
Bear Tales*
Lost & Found*
This Ads Up*
We're on the Write Note*
What's in a Name*

FOLLOWING DIRECTIONS
Bear Tales*
Over, Under, & Up
Pyramid Poetry
A Rainbow of Poetry
We're on the Write Note*

HYPERBOLE
All activities

IDIOMS and MULTIPLE MEANINGS
All Fired Up!
Bear Tales
Can of Worms*
Don't Be a Ding-a-Ling. Write!*
Hang by a Swinging Tale
Hats Off to Good Writing
Hop to It and Write!
In the Swim

Put Yourself in Our Shoes*
The Quilt Patch
The Upper Crust
We're on the Write Note
What's in a Name?
Write a Scooper-Dooper Story
Write Time
Writing — Rain or Shine

LETTER WRITING
All Fired Up!*
Can of Worms
In a Pickle
Lost & Found*

LIFE SKILLS
Bear Tales
Dial-a-Story*
Hang by a Swinging Tale*
The Quilt Patch*
Take Cover and Write*
This Ads Up
Writing — Rain or Shine

LIKENESSES and DIFFERENCES
All Fired Up!*
Food for Thought
Hop to It and Write!*
I'm in Hot Water Again*
In the Swim*
Lost & Found*
Pyramid Poetry
Unreal Estate
Writing — Rain or Shine

MAKING JUDGMENTS
Bear Tales
Can of Worms
Hop to It and Write!
I'm in Hot Water Again*
The Upper Crust*
Write a T-rrific Story*

MAP SKILLS
Write a Scooper-Dooper Story*
Write a T-rrific Story*

ONOMATOPOEIA
Hats Off to Good Writing
Hop to It and Write!
Put Yourself in Our Shoes
Stories To Fit You Like a Glove
We're on the Write Note
Write a Scooper-Dooper Story
Write a T-rrific Story

ORAL LANGUAGE DEVELOPMENT
Dial-a-Story*
Don't Be a Ding-a-Ling. Write!*
The Genie in My Thermos*
I'm in Hot Water Again*
In a Pickle*

PARTS of SPEECH
Over, Under, & Up
Pyramid Poetry

PERSONIFICATION
All Fired Up!
Dial-a-Story
Don't Be a Ding-a-Ling. Write!
Hats Off to Good Writing
Hop to It and Write!
The Quilt Patch
Stories To Fit You Like a Glove
Stories up Our Sleeves
We're on the Write Note
Write a T-rrific Story
Write Time
Writing — Rain or Shine

POINT of VIEW
All activities

PROBLEM SOLVING
All activities

QUOTATIONS and DIALOGUE
Dial-a-Story
Don't Be a Ding-a-Ling. Write!
I'm in Hot Water Again
In the Swim

REALISM and FANTASY
All activities

RESEARCH
All Fired Up!*
Bear Tales*
Don't Be a Ding-a-Ling. Write!*
Food for Thought*
Hang by a Swinging Tale*
I'm in Hot Water Again*
In a Pickle*
In the Swim*
Put Yourself in Our Shoes*
The Quilt Patch*
Stories To Fit You Like a Glove*
Stories up Our Sleeves*
The Upper Crust*
We're on the Write Note*
Write a Scooper-Dooper Story*
Write a T-rrific Story
Writing — Rain or Shine*

SEQUENCING
Dial-a-Story*
Over, Under, & Up
Pyramid Poetry
This Ads Up
Writing — Rain or Shine
   (flashback)